MEDICI BOOKS FOR CHILDREN

Costume through the

by Ella Bruce

© The Medici Society Ltd., London, 1979.   Printed in England.   SBN 85503 051 8.

THE ANCIENT BRITONS

When the Romans first settled in Britain in A.D. 43 they were met by people who dressed in a different way from themselves. The Romans had come from a warm country and the soldiers were clad in short tunics and had bare legs. In the cold damp climate of England it became more sensible to cover the legs and wear heavier clothing. In the picture opposite is a Roman soldier.

The men of Ancient Britain wore long trousers which were gathered and tied at the ankle, and leather shoes or boots. Sometimes they bound the legs with strips of wool or linen in a crosswise fashion like the man on the centre page. When the weather was warm they also wore a kind of sleeveless vest or went bare-backed. When it was cold they wore a belted tunic over the trousers, and over that a cloak that was sometimes lined with fur.

The women of rank had long dresses belted at the waist and cloaks which reached the ankles. They wove the sheep or goat's wool or flax on simple looms. They liked bright colours and got the dyes from various plants. They could not weave patterns other than simple stripes and checks. They were, however, very clever at making jewellery. Both men and women wore bracelets, brooches, necklaces and belt buckles made of precious metals and bone. A woman of high rank had a fillet of gold bound round her loose hair. A fillet is like a plain thin crown.

Some married ladies plaited their hair and wound it round their heads like the one shown on the centre page.

THE ANGLO SAXONS (about 500–1066)

The Romans had some influence on the way people dressed in Britain but styles did not alter a lot until the Saxons and Danes came to England. Then it became fashionable for both men and women to wear over-tunics. Under these were worn an under-tunic with long fitting sleeves. This was usually white or light in colour. On women it swept the ground, like the dress in the picture opposite. The man is still wearing the short tunic with long loose trousers gathered at the ankle into leather shoes. He also wears a cloak which is pinned at the front with a handsome brooch.

In those days a few people, the lords and thanes, lived in fortified houses, with the rest of the people living close by for protection. The lords and their wives and families often wore jewels on their belts and embroidered borders on their brightly coloured over-tunics.

The sketch on this page shows King Alfred as a boy, reading a book by the light of a candle which also served as a clock. Each ring on the candle represents an hour of time. Letters were written with a quill pen made from a goose feather on parchment, and rolled into a scroll like the one beside the candle.

MEDIEVAL (1066–1485)

When William of Normandy conquered England in 1066 the simple garments of the English people underwent some changes in detail, but throughout the Medieval period the general outline was more or less the same. Ladies' dresses were long and full, usually falling straight from a high waist. Sometimes the sleeves had long cuffs that reached the ground, like the one at the top of this page.

After years of hiding their hair beneath draperies women began to take a pride in showing it once more and, by adding false hair, wearing it in long plaits twisted or bound with ribbon, like the lower sketch on this page. Coronets, which were like little crowns, were worn over a light veil. Hair styles, and later headdresses, became very elaborate in the mid 15th century. One example is given in the picture opposite, and another on the title page.

Men wore tunics, either long to the ankles or short above the knees, over tight fitting hose. Like the women's head gear, their hats varied in shape and size. In the picture the gentleman is wearing a very popular style which lasted many years. The lady is wishing her husband luck before he goes coursing or hunting for hares with his dogs. Their home is a stone built Norman castle which, in the 15th century, would have been three hundred years old. Many of them are still standing today.

THE TUDORS (1485–1603)

The great Queen Elizabeth the First reigned in the 16th century, and by then the flowing lines of fashion had given way to a very stiff ornamental style of dress. Both men and women wore what were called ruffs round the neck, as in the picture opposite. They varied in size, at first rather small, but by the end of the century they had become huge and the women finally favoured large wired collars like the one in the lower sketch on this page, and on the cover.

A lot of padding was used in the sleeves and upper parts of men's hose. The padding was covered by a layer of silk beneath an outer layer, perhaps of satin, which was slashed to form ribbons. Ladies wore hoops beneath their skirts to make them stand out from the hips, and the garments of both sexes were often heavily embroidered.

Although the Elizabethan costume was very gay and full of colour it must have been most uncomfortable to wear, especially for children who were dressed similarly to their parents.

At the top of this page is an early Tudor lady, and at the bottom, a lady and gentleman, dressed in the later Tudor style, are dancing.

THE STUARTS (1603–1714)

The Stuarts reigned from 1603 to 1714 with an interval of eleven years in the middle, when kings were abolished as a result of the Civil War and Oliver Cromwell emerged as the ruler of the country. In these eleven years, known as the Commonwealth, elaborate clothes were thought extravagant and wicked, so that it was a dull time for fashion. But when the Stuart kings came back on to the throne many men and women returned to dressing in the elaborate manner of their forefathers.

On the opposite page is a picture of a mother and little daughter playing a game of hide-and-seek with father in the garden of their home. This is in the time of King Charles the Second when men cut their hair short and wore long curly wigs. They usually carried their hats, which were decorated with ostrich feathers, under their arms. Wigs, in a way, took the place of hats. Their clothes were colourful and were trimmed with lace and ribbons.

Women had their own hair dressed in different styles with soft shoulder length ringlets, but their clothes were not so flamboyant as the men's. The family in the picture are dressed in clothes of about 1670. For a few years ladies' dresses sometimes had a very low neckline which did not even cover the shoulders.

At the top of this page are two Puritans. Puritans were a group of religious people of this period who believed in simple living, and their clothes reflected their beliefs both in colour and design. At the bottom is a sketch of a typical street in London before the Great Fire which took place in 1666. The houses were made of wood and plaster and very easily burned to the ground.

THE HANOVERIANS (from 1714)

The first of the Hanoverian monarchs was George the First who came to the throne in 1714. Fashions had changed again since Stuart times. Now women's clothes tended to become more ornamental than men's with brighter colours, and their garments included embroidered silks and satins with lots of frills and flounces.

On the opposite page are a lady and gentleman in the portico of a big house in the 1720s. He has a rather elaborate coat and waistcoat and they both have powdered hair which was very fashionable, especially for the evening. Large gardens were very formal at that time, with low box hedges round the flower beds.

About 1770 women built their hair, still powdered, high up over cages and added the most fantastic articles by way of decoration, like the lady in the sketch on this page. Stuffed birds, ribbons, flowers, feathers and even models of ships might be perched upon this enormous coiffure. This fashion, however, did not last long, probably due to the fact that the discomfort outweighed the elegance it was supposed to create.

THE REGENCY (1810–1820)

The picture opposite is a scene of the Regency period. When George the Third, owing to illness, was no longer able to reign his son took over his duties and was called the Prince Regent—hence the name Regency. When his father died the Prince Regent inherited the throne and became George the Fourth.

You can see at a glance how fashion has changed. The women's waists are now high and the dresses based on the style worn by the Ancient Greeks. They were made of very flimsy materials so that even indoors a kind of short tunic was often worn over the dress. Outdoor coats were of heavier cloth. For a time ladies cut their hair short very like some of the styles of today. But they did not have the advantage of a perm so had to use heated irons to make the ends curly, as shown in the sketch above. As fashion changed and the hair was allowed to grow, it was tied up on top of the head leaving some curls hanging down on either side of the face, a forerunner of mid-Victorian hairdressing.

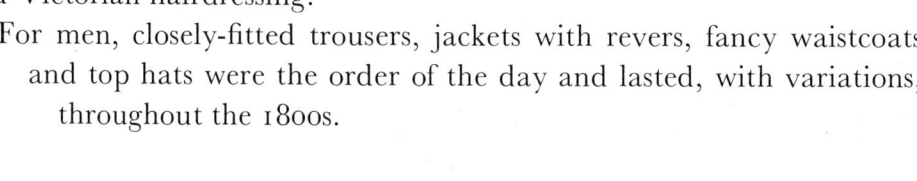

For men, closely-fitted trousers, jackets with revers, fancy waistcoats and top hats were the order of the day and lasted, with variations, throughout the 1800s.

THE VICTORIANS (1837–1901)

Soon after the Regency period women's skirts became fuller. Sleeves were puffed out at the top making the shoulders wider, and larger hats were worn. Skirts were cut shorter to show the ankles, and boots were worn for the first time by ladies. The style of men's clothes became more square in outline, as you will see in the sketch at the top of this page.

By the 1860s when Queen Victoria was well established on the throne fashion in women's wear had drastically changed again. On the opposite page is a lady of this period reading the contents of a letter to a visitor. See how the skirts have become fuller still and once more reach the ground. They are worn over a cage of hoops to make them stick out. The hoops were made of whalebone and could easily be bent to pass through a narrow doorway. All the same, in a Victorian room overloaded with ornaments and heavy furniture they must have been very difficult to manoeuvre. Over the cage were worn four or more frilly petticoats and the dress itself was most likely made of velvet or plush, adding weight and heat to the poor wearer. The bold ornamentation of braid and the contrasting crude colours, even in outdoor clothes, made this a very gay period in the matter of dress. Aniline dyes made from coal tar had been recently discovered and gave an almost unlimited range of bright colours reasonably fast to light.

Towards the end of the century there were big changes in men's clothes, particularly for games and sports. The straw hat was seen for the first time on the river and at the seaside and top hats were no longer worn for cricket. Little tweed caps became popular.

Also, by the end of the century hoops had disappeared from skirts and the bustle took over like the one at the bottom of this page worn by the lady playing croquet. You will notice how the hair is now tightly scraped up into a bunch of curls high over the forehead.

THE EDWARDIANS (1901–1910)

By the time Edward the Seventh came to the throne in 1901 there was a great change on the roads of Britain. The motor car had arrived and bicycling had become popular with both sexes.

Ladies had acquired another new shape—in silhouette rather like an hour glass, pinched in to a very small waist, the skirt flaring out like a bell below and the full sleeves giving width above. Some sleeves used far more material above the elbow than in the bodice itself, and these were called "leg-of-mutton" sleeves. But the lady in the picture opposite lived a few years later, when the sleeves were not so extreme and the skirts had more fullness at the back than at the front and trailed on the ground. However these clothes could not be used when riding a bicycle. The skirt would soon have caught in the wheels and caused an accident, so a kind of masculine suit was designed for the purpose and the ladies wore knickerbockers. These were like loose trousers gathered into stockings below the knees and sometimes covered by a short flared skirt, like the one in the sketch at the top of this page. A shirt blouse, which first came into fashion at this time, a straw hat and perhaps a short jacket completed the outfit.

For motoring a veil was tied over the ladies' wide brimmed hats as at first there was no cover to the car, and heavy capes kept the driver and his passengers warm. The car on the opposite page has broken down on its way to the big house. The owner of the house has come with his daughter to meet the visitors and is trying to help by turning the starting handle. You will see that he is wearing a knickerbocker suit made of tweed. Country clothes for men were by now quite different from those worn in town.

THE 1920s TO 1960

By the 1920s women, who had undertaken so many men's jobs during World War I, had become much more independent and took an active part in work and games. They no longer wanted to be laden with a lot of unnecessary clothing. So, step by step, after the Edwardian age, they discarded all that was uncomfortable and finally arrived at the simple dress of the twenties. You will notice on the opposite page that the small waist is missing. In fact there is no waist at all. Sometimes a sash or belt was placed round the hips but the general outline was like a box, straight from shoulder to hem. Usually the skirt came just below the knees but there were variations in dance and evening wear when the hemline became uneven, dipping at the back or sides.

The two tennis players are wearing typical sports dresses giving them the freedom of movement which no woman had ever had before. They also cut their hair short. If not "bobbed" as it was called, the hair was parted in the middle, plaited and wound over the ears. The two styles are shown in the picture. The men wore white open-necked shirts and wide flannel trousers.

The sketch at the bottom of this page shows a woman in the Royal Air Force costume during World War II talking to a civilian in a dress of the time when even clothes rationing was necessary. Two years after the drab period of the war women could buy as many clothes as they could afford and fashion dropped the hemline almost to the ankles and called it the "New Look". But this vogue did not last long.

At the top of this page is a crinoline dress of the late 1950s worn over a full starched petticoat.

THE 1960s AND 1970s

In the 1960s the mini skirt appeared. It was essentially for the young. The not so young wore their skirts just above the knees. By the early 1970s full freedom of expression in clothes had been attained. Women could now wear what suited them or took their fancy. During the war they had begun wearing trousers for comfort and utility and they gradually became part of everyday dress. When clad in denim jeans and having similar hair styles, men and women tended to look alike.